The Seldom-Ever-Shady Glades

POEMS AND QUILTS BY

Sue Van Wassenhove

WORDSONG
Honesdale, Pennsylvania

In memory of my quilting mom, Jean Larson

J 811.6
Van Wassenhove

ACKNOWLEDGMENTS

Thanks to the Miami Children's Writing Group for encouraging me to take my writing seriously; Christie Jones, curator of palms and cycads, Fairchild Tropical Botanic Gardens, Coral Gables, Florida; and Dieter Van Wassenhove for his patient computer guidance. Many thanks to my editor, Joan Hyman, and the designer, Mina Greenstein, for their guidance and support in the creation of this book.—S.V.W.

The publisher thanks Dr. John H. Rappole, an ornithologist with the Smithsonian National Zoological Park, Conservation and Research Center, and a member of the board of directors of the Roger Tory Peterson Institute, for reviewing the poetry.

Wordsong
An Imprint of Boyds Mills Press, Inc.
815 Church Street, Honesdale, Pennsylvania 18431
Printed in China

First edition
Book design by Mina Greenstein and Sue Van Wassenhove
The text of this book is set in 14-point Quorum Bold.
The illustrations are quilts.

10 9 8 7 6 5 4 3 2 1

Library of Congress Cataloging-in-Publication Data
Van Wassenhove, Sue.
  The seldom-ever-shady glades / by Sue Van Wassenhove.
    p. cm.
  ISBN-13: 978-1-59078-352-8 (hardcover : alk. paper)
  1. Birds—Juvenile poetry. 2. Animals—Juvenile poetry.
  3. Nature—Juvenile poetry. 4. Everglades (Fla.)—Juvenile poetry.
  5. Children's poetry, American. I. Title.
  PS3622.A5858S46 2008
  811'.6—dc22
                                            2007018099

Contents

The Seldom-Ever-Shady Glades

The seldom-ever-shady Glades loves birds with panache,
a paradise for waders, if their passion's saw grass.
The splashers in the bladey Glades, just passing the day,
crocs and gators salivating over sashaying prey.

The better wait-er gator eats a heron for lunch.
The better wait-er gator grabs a gar he can munch.
He doesn't have to move much, sunning, waiting for snacks.
The better wait-er gator, hear those crab legs crack!

The fling-a-wing anhinga dives to make the schools dance.
He suns his feathered fing-ahs, has a bill like a lance.
He tosses skewered fishies that he swallows head first.
Please tell me, Sir Anhinga, how your gullet doesn't burst.

The magnificent frigate is a bird, not a boat.
This pirate of the trade winds sports a fork-tailed black coat.
His hooked bill steals from boobies, snatches fish that can fly.
The magnificent frigate bird dines low but flies high.

The rosy tutu spoonbill chooses food in the mud.
Ballerina legs and body, but a face like a spud.
Her flat beak feels the water, swishing, "No, no, no!"
scooping back and forth for tasty shrimp and fish that move slow.

5

The soft-shelled elder turtle has a tube for a snout.
Her cousins sun their toesies with their feet stretched out.
Known as bellied sliders, they're in yellow or red,
and all three of these turtles have a house they can't shed.

The cormorant that's crested has a mouth that turns blue.
It's mating-ladies tested; it's the best he can do.
He dives to find his supper, then he suns his wings dry.
Did the cormorant that's crested gargle bright blue dye?

The great blue starin' heron yellow-eyeballs his prey.
Time is not his issue: he can wait the whole day.
He's ducktail slick and tailored, tucks his curved neck S-tigh
The great blue starin' heron has a cousin that's white.

6

The black dabbly skimmer drags his lip in the sea.
He dips for surface swimmers he can slurp for high tea.
His lower jaw is bigger than his red legs are long.
The profile of the skimmer proves he's mandibly strong.

The overeater skeeter—a sweet greeter he ain't.
While other critters scatter, he sticks close as wet paint.
Depleted hoards in winter grow to swarms in June heat.
Bloodthirsty as the panther, with a bite more discreet.

The river of the Everglades flows south to the bay.
There, manatees and snakebirds swim a water ballet.
Please help preserve this treasure lying north of the Keys.
Maybe nature lasts forever, but there's no guarantee.

Change of Seasons

When the parched wind passes,
    spring tinder grasses
    must burn or die.
When old gators guard mudholes
    nearly dry . . .
When herons must fly
    far for fish . . .

Then cloud towers bloom proud
    during June afternoons.
Growling thunder booms loud
    as heat shimmers at noon.
Soon the sweet rains gain power
    as the wet season grows.
By September fall showers
    make low creeks overflow.

Then wild winds hiss
    and whiplash the saw grass.
Wrenching gray rains
    drench and swamp so fast
even ibises flee
    from the hurricane's face.
But the Glades take the fury
    with favor and grace.

Those wisp-bottomed gray clouds
yearn to drop rain.
And the crackling grass, thirsty,
reaches in vain,
'cause the naughty winds playfully
toy with them both,
tossing the helpless clouds
out past the coast.

Still Dry

9

Standoff

The heron spreads his wings and flies away.
His nighttime perch sits high above the Glades,
where alligators prowl and grasses sway.

When egrets and rose spoonbills all display
for mates, they wade and prance in proud parades.
The heron spreads his wings and flies away;

this feathered group, too handy a buffet
for razor teeth lined up like saw-grass blades
in alligator jowls. When grasses sway,

the great blue knows the gator's stalking prey.
Just out of reach, aloof and undismayed,
the heron preens his wings and turns away.

A pair of surfaced periscopes betrays
the gray below the water in the shade.
This alligator scowls and grasses sway.

So birds assess the gator's right-of-way,
and if they sense a fishing-hole blockade,
the heron spreads his wings and flies away.
Where alligators prowl, trespassers pay.

Professor Heron

Our Professor,
the great blue.
That black, slicked-back hairpiece
and subtle, mottled cravat
hide his bony neck.
A dusty, gray tweed jacket
with rusty academic shoulders and elbows
tops long, lock-kneed legs
and polished wing tips.
But his yellow-eyed stare
and gripped, tight-lipped silence
can outwait
any
squirming indignities
we try to submerge.

The Heron Blues

The great blue is tall,
and the little is small.
But the little is blue,
and the great ain't, that's true.
Would you choose
the same names?

The little blue heron is nearly all blue, including its beak.
The great blue heron is mostly gray.

13

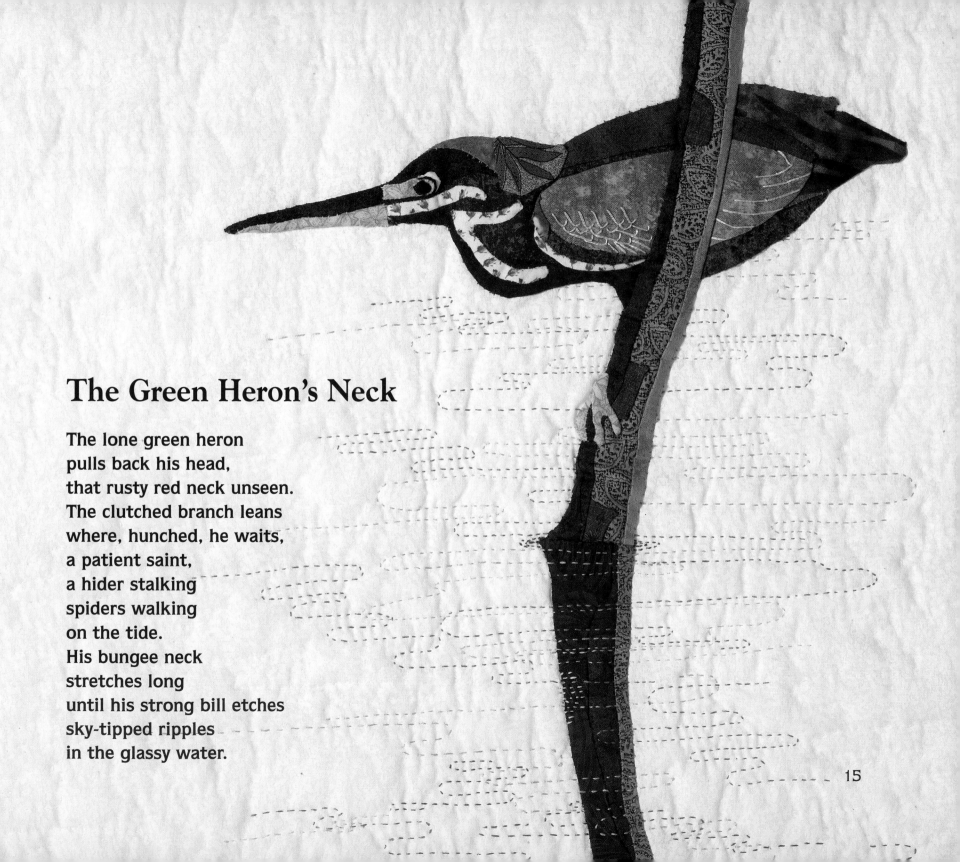

The Green Heron's Neck

The lone green heron
pulls back his head,
that rusty red neck unseen.
The clutched branch leans
where, hunched, he waits,
a patient saint,
a hider stalking
spiders walking
on the tide.
His bungee neck
stretches long
until his strong bill etches
sky-tipped ripples
in the glassy water.

15

Cormorant Amour

The cormorant hot dude,
to pick from spring chicks,
though certainly not rude,
just can't hide his tricks.

Those winks edged in turquoise,
his emerald eyes
stare like he's berserk. Boy,
restraint would be wise!

By damsels bedeviled,
he sprouts temple tufts.
Now double disheveled,
he's crested enough

to wind-toss his feathers—
so biker-bird cool.
When gals flock together,
he tries not to drool.

His orange mouth hangs open,
though hardly for flies.
It's his throat that he's hopin'
will show he's a prize.

Girls, check out that gullet!
Look deep down his throat!
Yes, even his palate's
a tempting new coat

of blue! He pants harder
to show he's of age.
For cormorant ardor,
blues must be the rage.

Keeping Clean

With help from bleach and wash machines,
a mom might keep her girl's frills clean.
But both know that they challenge fate
by dressing her all white, in lace.
They dare the elements, which scheme
to spoil her clothes before she's seen.

By nature white, the egret fondly
trails his long lace in the pond,
then twists to groom it with his beak
and drags it wet when he must eat.
Yet with no mom to intervene,
somehow his plumes remain pristine.

The great egret grows beautiful, long
plumes during breeding season.

19

Snowy Egrets

Dressed in frilled tails,
elegantly white,
with black spats tight
over yellow patent shoes,
the snowy two
circle each other
like skater-lovers.
Wings beat their dance
past green and gold plants,
all mirrored in the dark
morning water of the park.
Yellow toes dip, not too deep,
to trick fish to leap
from waters so still.
Both thin, black bills
will needle a meal,
then wheel to the trees
to preen plumes in the breeze.

Snowy egrets are small with white
feathers. Their black legs have bright
yellow feet. Some snowies frighten
fish by dragging their feet in the
water as they fly. When the fish jump
into the air, the birds grab them and
fly their meals to the trees.

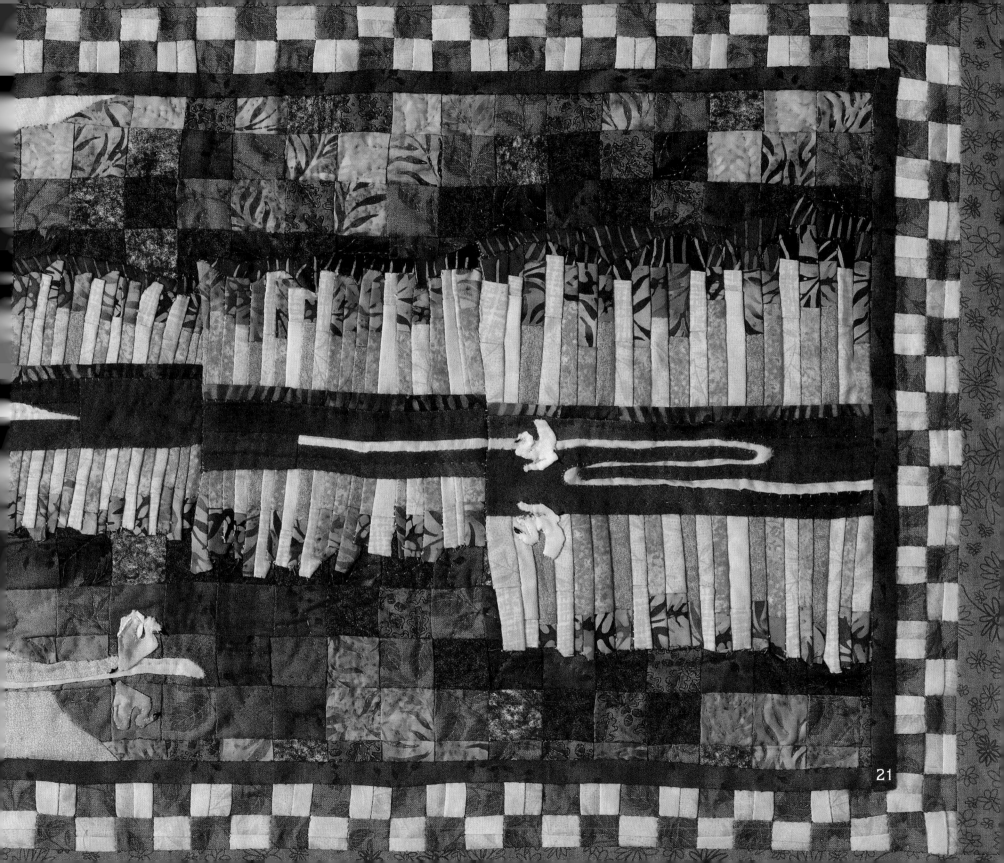

21

The Florida Keys
grow canopies
of mangrove trees
for manatees.

And Portuguese
sea men-of-war
patrol the shore.
Oh, don't you wish
moon jellyfish
had jelly bellies?
Weren't so smelly?
Had no stringy
things that sting?

Grief is perching
on the reef
if you lurch
on ocean urchins.

Below the Keys' Seas

Also lurking
in the bay,
the eagle ray—
flat, gray, and wide
with spots to hide
its rippling glide.

Beneath the tide
beware!
The barracuda's dash,
a silver flash
below the waves.

Souls brave enough
to swim with him
face chances slimmer,
grimmer still
when waters, chill,
fill in with sharks.

23

The tricolor heron, one of the smaller herons in the Everglades, can fish on the fly from low branches along the water.

The Tiny Shy Tri

It's amazing
the tiny, shy tri
can find fish each day.

Its squawking
fly cry
should scare fish away.

But each flapping
spry try
snags a fish as its pay.

The Mockingbird's Repertoire

How fancy-free the jubilee
of tunes sung by the mockingbird.
His serenade, a concert made
of secret strains he overheard.

When birds were new, before they flew,
God whispered each a melody.
Most didn't stay, but flew away
to sing their song from every tree.

The mockingbird, the last conferred,
rewarded for his patient ear,
may now recite as his birthright
those precious songs he longed to hear.

Some northern mockingbirds,
Florida's state bird, have been
recorded singing more than
a hundred different tunes.

Royal Palms

Along the summer avenue
the royal palms pose tall and bold.
Imposing forms, each poised and paused
in perfect unison. All hold

the third position, ankles crossed.
Their daily ballet discipline:
to line the street, knees locked, legs straight.
Stiff-crimped and crinkled crinolines

show off slim hips and slender waists.
A ruffled spray of fine fruit beads
gives tutus sparkle in the sun.
But high on top, all movement's freed.

Long, graceful, arching palms undone,
arms sweep the sky. Green fronds unpinned
to toss their crowns, with hair unbunned,
they dance the rhythms of the wind.

Anhinga Flings

And another anhinga
in the hinterglades
unhinges its wings
after animated angling,
flinging for any hint
of drying sun.

28

The anhinga, or snakebird, is an excellent swimmer that eats fish. However, since it has no oil gland to keep its feathers dry, it must spread its wings and air-dry them.

Bird Watching

You must search along the shorelines
on arched mangroves before evening,
or you'll miss the sly green heron,
miss the snowies, miss the grebe.

Check if hidden in the saw grass
and tall reeds along the creek bed,
you can spot the tan-streaked bittern
stretch his neck or hear his tread.

You should sit beside the willows,
watch for flutters in the sunlight,
or you'll miss the yellow warblers,
black-crowned herons awaiting night.

You must watch the water's surface
for the splashing of the culler,
or you'll miss the whistling osprey
dive with pelicans and gulls.

Don't forget to look above you
for the wood stork circling higher.
You could miss the passing spoonbill,
miss the egret, miss the kite.

You must listen, long and patient,
for the red-winged blackbird's ballad.
You might miss woodpecker chatter
and the oriole's chorale.

Try to find the springtime fledglings,
hatchlings peeping in the thicket.
You might catch new ducklings line up
or a moorhen feed her chicks.

You should take the time to see them.
If you don't attend their thronging,
know the world will turn without you,
but your soul might miss God's song.

Night Cousins

Crowned black or yellow, these two birds
hunch in the day: Do Not Disturb.

One strutting butler, black and white,
officiates the Glades by night.

His cousin, spruced up in his best
flamboyant feather cloak and vest,

festoons his back with pale head plumes.
This heron-baron makes chicks swoon.

When dawn floods light across the skies,
it's shut-eye time for black-tie guys.

Black-crowned night herons and yellow-crowned night herons
are mainly nocturnal birds, though yellow-crowns' foraging
habits are influenced by the tides.